Audio Access Included

PLAYBACK+
Speed • Pitch • Balance • Loop

Teaching Little Fingers to Play
More Movie Music

10 Piano Solos with Optional Accompaniments arranged by
Carolyn Miller

Includes Online Audio

Orchestrations by Eric Baumgartner

Each piece includes two audio tracks: one with both piano and orchestration at a practice tempo, and one with just the orchestration at a faster performance tempo. With our exclusive **Playback+** feature, you can change the tempo even more without altering the pitch, plus set loop points for continuous repetition of tricky measures.

To access audio visit:
www.halleonard.com/mylibrary

Enter Code
6733-0525-7589-8550

ISBN 978-1-4950-0634-0

WILLIS MUSIC

EXCLUSIVELY DISTRIBUTED BY

HAL•LEONARD®
CORPORATION
7777 W. BLUEMOUND RD. P.O. BOX 13819 MILWAUKEE, WI 53213

Visit Hal Leonard Online at
www.halleonard.com

CONTENTS

True Love's Kiss

from Walt Disney Pictures' ENCHANTED

Optional Accompaniment

Music by Alan Menken
Lyrics by Stephen Schwartz
Arranged by Carolyn Miller

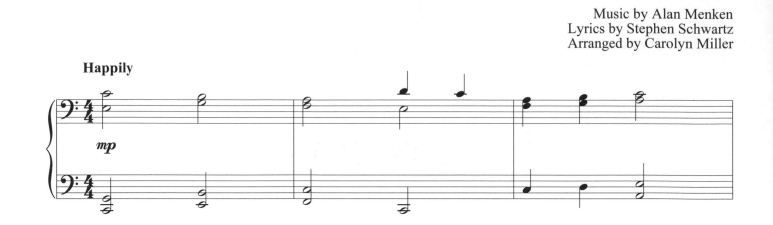

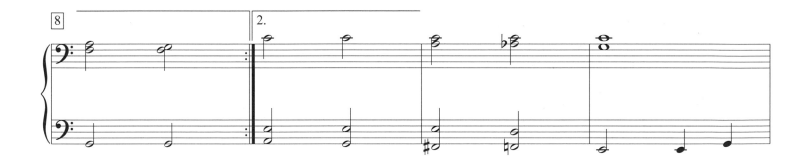

True Love's Kiss

from Walt Disney Pictures' ENCHANTED

Music by Alan Menken
Lyrics by Stephen Schwartz
Arranged by Carolyn Miller

Play both hands one octave higher when performing as a duet.

Forrest Gump – Main Title

(Feather Theme)

from the Paramount Motion Picture FORREST GUMP

Optional Accompaniment

Music by Alan Silvestri
Arranged by Carolyn Miller

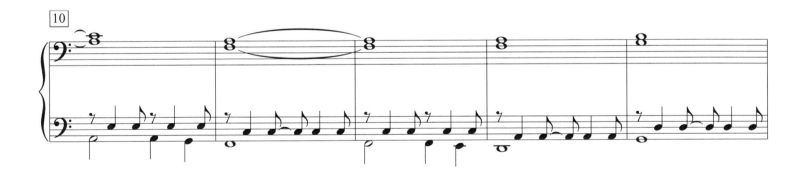

Forrest Gump – Main Title

(Feather Theme)

from the Paramount Motion Picture FORREST GUMP

Music by Alan Silvestri
Arranged by Carolyn Miller

Play both hands one octave higher when performing as a duet.

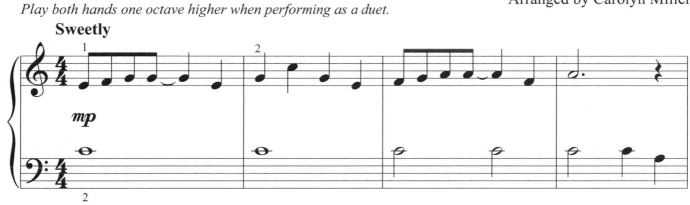

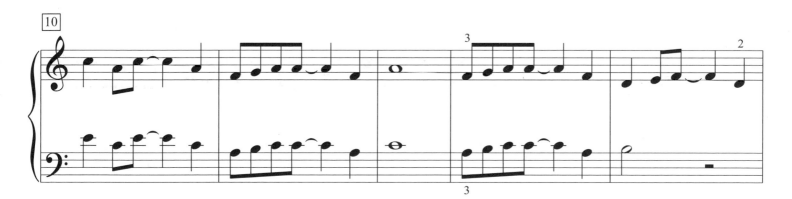

I See the Light

from Walt Disney Pictures' TANGLED

Optional Accompaniment

Music by Alan Menken
Lyrics by Glenn Slater
Arranged by Carolyn Miller

I See the Light
from Walt Disney Pictures' TANGLED

Music by Alan Menken
Lyrics by Glenn Slater
Arranged by Carolyn Miller

Play both hands one octave higher when performing as a duet.

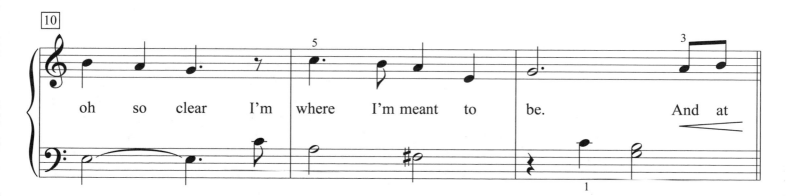

Accompaniment

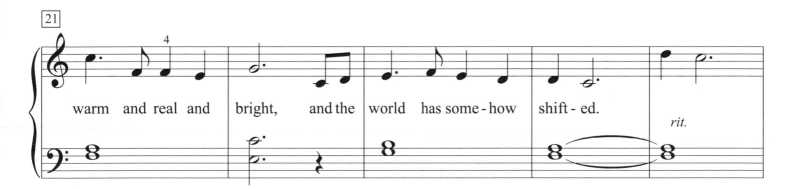

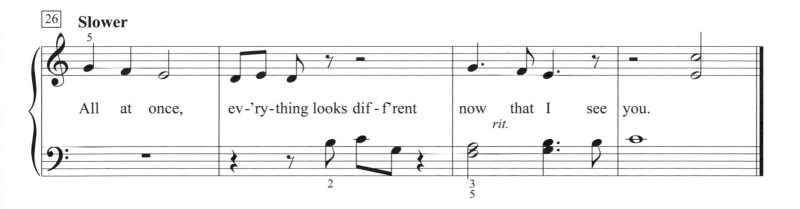

Somewhere Out There

from AN AMERICAN TAIL

Optional Accompaniment

Music by Barry Mann and James Horner
Lyric by Cynthia Weil
Arranged by Carolyn Miller

Somewhere Out There
from AN AMERICAN TAIL

Music by Barry Mann and James Horner
Lyric by Cynthia Weil
Arranged by Carolyn Miller

Play both hands one octave higher when performing as a duet.

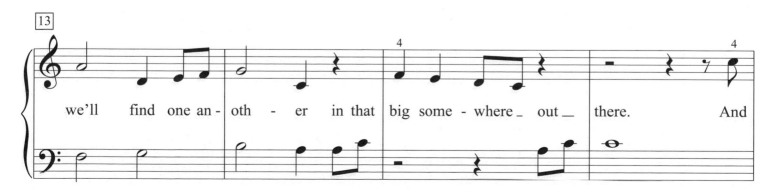

Accompaniment

e - ven though I know how ver - y   far a - part we are,   it   helps to think we might be wish- in'

on the same bright star.   And when the night wind starts to sing a   lone-some lull - a - by,   it

helps to think we're sleep-ing un - der - neath the same big   sky. Some - where

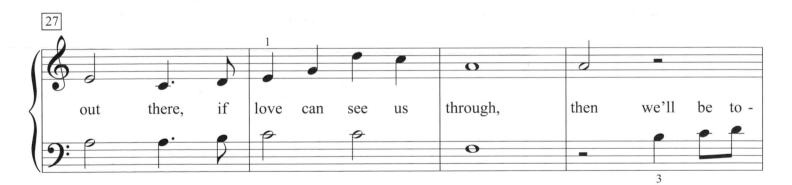

out   there, if love can see us   through,   then   we'll be to -

geth - er, some-where out there,   out where dreams come   true.

Moon River
from the Paramount Picture BREAKFAST AT TIFFANY'S

Optional Accompaniment

Words by Johnny Mercer
Music by Henry Mancini
Arranged by Carolyn Miller

Moon River
from the Paramount Picture BREAKFAST AT TIFFANY'S

Words by Johnny Mercer
Music by Henry Mancini
Arranged by Carolyn Miller

Play both hands one octave higher when performing as a duet.

Accompaniment

rit.

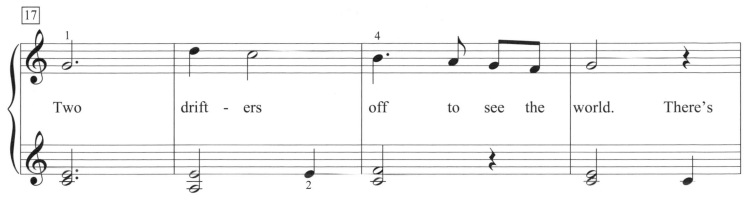

Two drift - ers off to see the world. There's

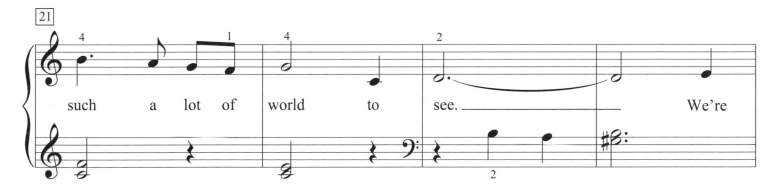

such a lot of world to see. _____ We're

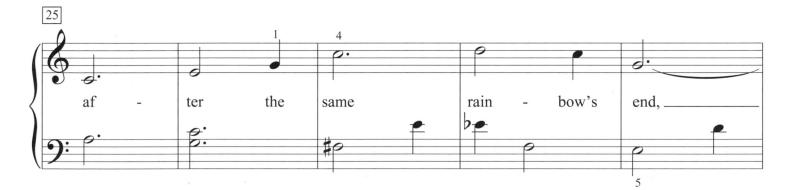

af - ter the same rain - bow's end, _____

_____ wait - in' 'round the bend, _____ my Huck - le - ber - ry friend,

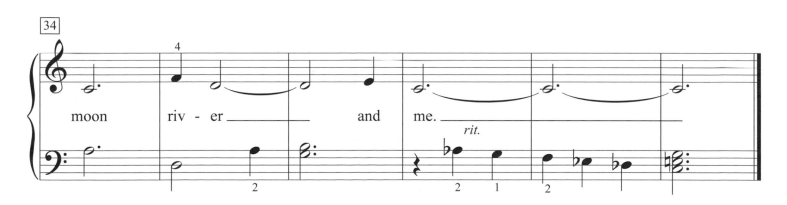

moon riv - er _____ and me. _____
rit.

Let It Grow
(Celebrate the World)
from the Motion Picture THE LORAX

Optional Accompaniment

Music and Lyrics by Ester Dean,
Christopher "Tricky" Stewart,
John Powell, Cinco Paul and Aaron Pearce
Arranged by Carolyn Miller

With energy

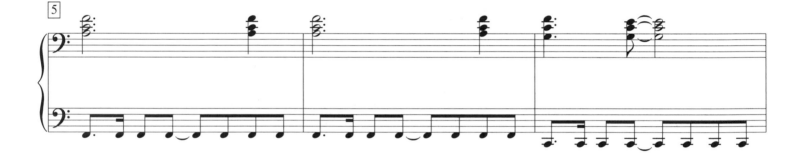

Let It Grow
(Celebrate the World)
from the Motion Picture THE LORAX

Music and Lyrics by Ester Dean,
Christopher "Tricky" Stewart,
John Powell, Cinco Paul and Aaron Pearce
Arranged by Carolyn Miller

Play both hands one octave higher when performing as a duet.

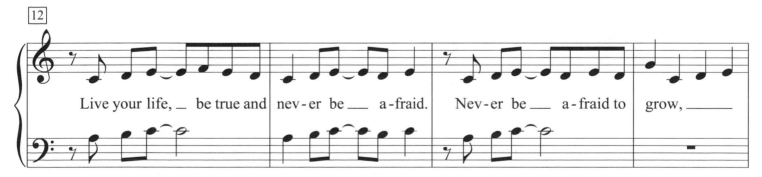

Accompaniment

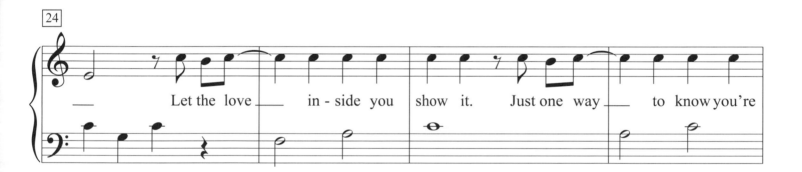

Bella's Lullaby

from the Summit Entertainment film TWILIGHT

Optional Accompaniment

Composed by Carter Burwell
Arranged by Carolyn Miller

Bella's Lullaby

from the Summit Entertainment film TWILIGHT

Composed by Carter Burwell
Arranged by Carolyn Miller

Play both hands one octave higher when performing as a duet.

Moderately

Accompaniment

The Pink Panther

from THE PINK PANTHER

Optional Accompaniment

By Henry Mancini
Arranged by Carolyn Miller

Mysterioso, with a swing feel

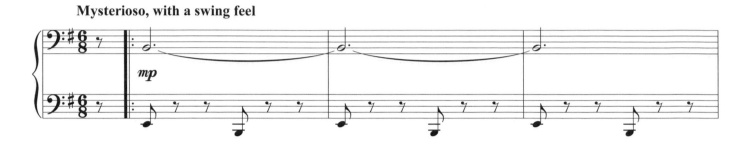

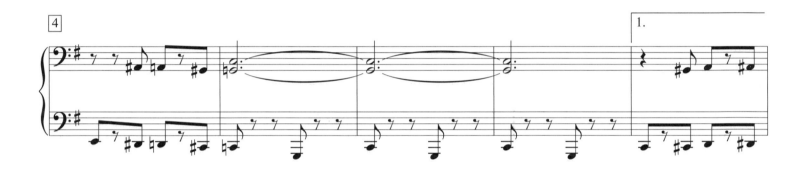

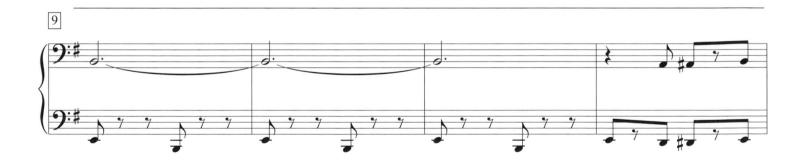

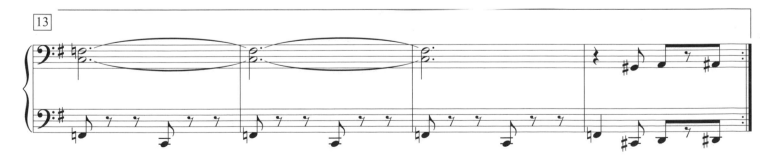

The Pink Panther
from THE PINK PANTHER

By Henry Mancini
Arranged by Carolyn Miller

Play both hands one octave higher when performing as a duet.

Mysterioso, with a swing feel

Accompaniment

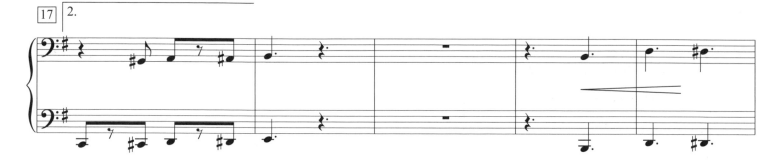

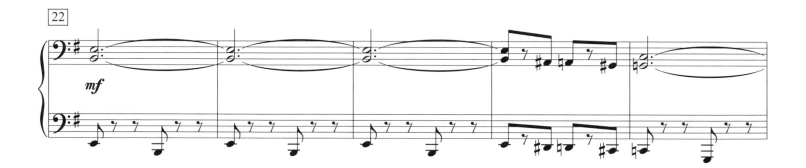

The Sound of Music
from THE SOUND OF MUSIC

Optional Accompaniment

Lyrics by Oscar Hammerstein II
Music by Richard Rodgers
Arranged by Carolyn Miller

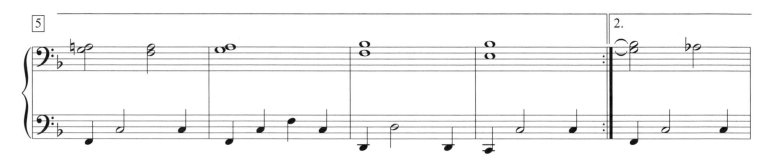

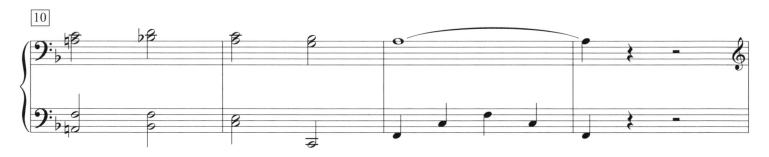

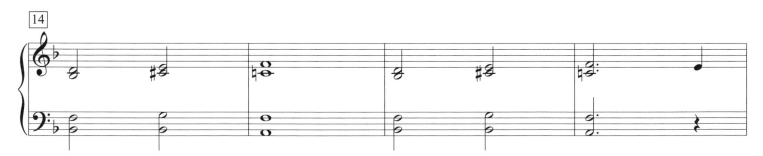

The Sound of Music
from THE SOUND OF MUSIC

Lyrics by Oscar Hammerstein II
Music by Richard Rodgers
Arranged by Carolyn Miller

Play both hands one octave higher when performing as a duet.

Accompaniment

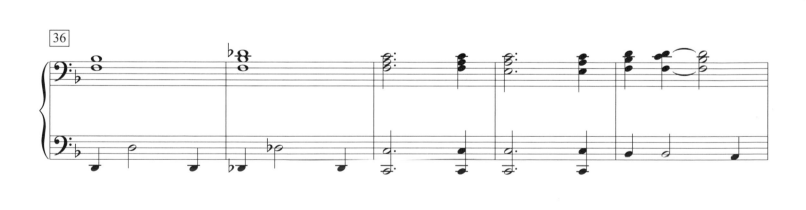

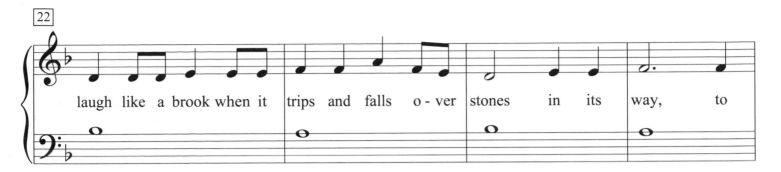

laugh like a brook when it trips and falls o-ver stones in its way, to

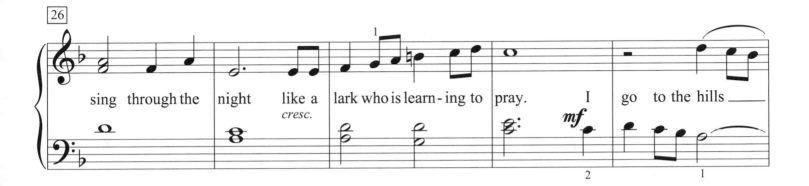

sing through the night like a lark who is learn-ing to pray. I go to the hills

when my heart is lone-ly. I know I will hear what I've heard be-

fore. My heart will be blessed with the sound of mu - sic

and I'll sing once more.

Summer Nights

from GREASE

Optional Accompaniment

Lyric and Music by
Warren Casey and Jim Jacobs
Arranged by Carolyn Miller

Moderato

Summer Nights
from GREASE

Lyric and Music by
Warren Casey and Jim Jacobs
Arranged by Carolyn Miller

Play both hands one octave higher when performing as a duet.

38

Accompaniment

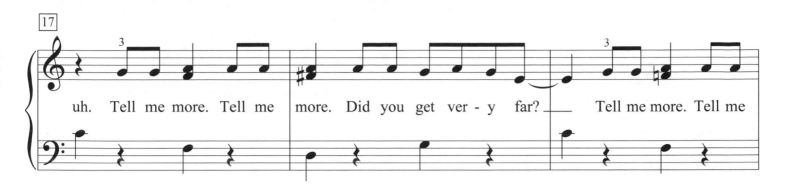

TEACHING LITTLE FINGERS TO PLAY MORE

TEACHING LITTLE FINGERS TO PLAY MORE
by Leigh Kaplan

Teaching Little Fingers to Play More is a fun-filled and colorfully illustrated follow-up book to *Teaching Little Fingers to Play*. It strengthens skills learned while carefully easing the transition into John Thompson's *Modern Course, First Grade*.

00406137 Book only $6.99
00406527 Book/CD $9.99

SUPPLEMENTARY SERIES
All books include optional teacher accompaniments.

BROADWAY SONGS
arr. Carolyn Miller
EARLY ELEMENTARY LEVEL
10 great show tunes for students to enjoy, including: Edelweiss • I Whistle a Happy Tune • I Won't Grow Up • Maybe • The Music of the Night • and more.
00416926 Book only $7.99
00416927 Book/CD $12.99

CHILDREN'S SONGS
arr. Carolyn Miller
MID-ELEMENTARY LEVEL
10 songs: The Candy Man • Do-Re-Mi • I'm Popeye the Sailor Man • It's a Small World • Linus and Lucy • The Muppet Show Theme • Sesame Street Theme • Supercalifragilisticexpialidocious • Tomorrow.
00416810 Book only $6.99
00416811 Book/CD $12.99

CLASSICS
arr. Randall Hartsell
MID-ELEMENTARY LEVEL
7 solos: Marche Slave • Over the Waves • Polovtsian Dance (from the opera *Prince Igor*) • Pomp and Circumstance • Rondeau • Waltz (from the ballet *Sleeping Beauty*) • William Tell Overture.
00406760 Book only $5.99
00416513 Book/CD $10.99

DISNEY TUNES
arr. Glenda Austin
MID-ELEMENTARY LEVEL
9 songs, including: Circle of Life • Colors of the Wind • A Dream Is a Wish Your Heart Makes • A Spoonful of Sugar • Under the Sea • A Whole New World • and more.
00416750 Book only $7.99
00416751 Book/CD $12.99

EASY DUETS
arr. Carolyn Miller
MID-ELEMENTARY LEVEL
9 equal-level duets: A Bicycle Built for Two • Blow the Man Down • Chopsticks • Do Your Ears Hang Low? • I've Been Working on the Railroad • The Man on the Flying Trapeze • Short'nin' Bread • Skip to My Lou • The Yellow Rose of Texas.
00416832 Book only $6.99
00416833 Book/CD $10.99

JAZZ AND ROCK
Eric Baumgartner
MID-ELEMENTARY LEVEL
11 solos, including: Big Bass Boogie • Crescendo Rock • Funky Fingers • Jazz Waltz in G • Rockin' Rhythm • Squirrel Race • and more!
00406765 Book only $5.99

MOVIE MUSIC
arr. Carolyn Miller
LATER ELEMENTARY LEVEL
10 magical movie arrangements: Bella's Lullaby (Twilight) • Somewhere Out There (An American Tail) • True Love's Kiss (Enchanted) • and more.
00139190 Book/Online Audio $10.99

Also available:

AMERICAN TUNES
arr. Eric Baumgartner
MID-ELEMENTARY LEVEL
00406755 Book only $5.99

BLUES AND BOOGIE
Carolyn Miller
MID-ELEMENTARY LEVEL
00406764 Book only $5.99

CHRISTMAS CAROLS
arr. Carolyn Miller
MID-ELEMENTARY LEVEL
00406763 Book only $5.99
00416475 Book/CD $10.99

CHRISTMAS CLASSICS
arr. Eric Baumgartner
MID-ELEMENTARY LEVEL
00416827 Book only $6.99
00416826 Book/CD $12.99

CHRISTMAS FAVORITES
arr. Eric Baumgartner
MID-ELEMENTARY LEVEL
00416723 Book only $7.99
00416724 Book/CD $12.99

FAMILIAR TUNES
arr. Glenda Austin
MID-ELEMENTARY LEVEL
00406761 Book only $5.99

HYMNS
arr. Glenda Austin
MID-ELEMENTARY LEVEL
00406762 Book only $5.99

JEWISH FAVORITES
arr. Eric Baumgartner
MID-ELEMENTARY LEVEL
00416755 Book only $5.99

RECITAL PIECES
Carolyn Miller
MID-ELEMENTARY LEVEL
00416540 Book only $5.99

SONGS FROM MANY LANDS
arr. Carolyn C. Setliff
MID-ELEMENTARY LEVEL
00416688 Book only $5.99